THE OFFICIAL

TOTTENHAM HOTSPUR

ANNUAL 2014

Written by Michael Bridge

Designed by Mathew Whittles

A Grange Publication

©2013. Published by Grange Communications Ltd., Edinburgh, under licence from Tottenham Hotspur Ltd. Printed in the EU.

Photography © Action Images & Shutterstock

ISBN 978 1

£7.99

WELCOME

Dear Supporters

Welcome to the Official Tottenham Hotspur Annual 2014.

In the following pages, you'll find a comprehensive 2012/2013 season review and an in-depth look into our squad, plus all you need to know about the rising stars of the Lane.

We broke a number of Club records last season – victory over Sunderland saw us achieve our greatest Premier League points tally ever. We also won 10 away League matches and had a good run in the Europa League, reaching the quarter-finals.

The new season promises to be even better, following our exciting summer signings: Nacer Chadli, Paulinho, Etienne Capoue, Roberto Soldado, Christian Eriksen, Vlad Chiriches and Erik Lamela.

Meet the team, test yourself in the quiz section and find out just why we are so unique. Remember, in a world of Uniteds, Citys and Rovers ... there is only One Hotspur.

Enjoy your new Annual.

Come on you Spurs!

PREMIER LEAGUE REVIEW 2012/2013

The 2012/2013 Season was another exciting campaign for Tottenham Hotspur, packed full of goals, great victories, and moments of individual brilliance. Spurs finished 5th under Head Coach Andre Villas-Boas with our Barclays Premier League record total of 72 points.

AUGUST

Pld: 2 W: 0 D: 1 L: 1
End of month Position: 14th

Our first match of the season ended in disappointment as a late Hatem Ben Arfa penalty earned all three points for Newcastle at St James' Park. The home side went ahead on 54 minutes through a wonder goal from Demba Ba. Spurs levelled through Jermain Defoe on 76 minutes, but Ben Arfa's penalty denied us a deserved share of the spoils. West Brom were the first visitors to White Hart Lane. Benoit Assou-Ekotto put Spurs ahead with a deflected 25-yard shot, but West Brom secured a point with James Morrison's stoppage time goal.

SEPTEMBER

Pld: 4 W: 3 D: 1 L: 0
End of month Position: 5th

Spurs were still searching for their first win against Norwich after Robert Snodgrass fired home a late equaliser. Mousa Dembele, on his debut, put Spurs ahead on 68 minutes, but the Canaries left with a point on another frustrating afternoon. Three points finally arrived in a deserved win at Reading, Jermain Defoe (2) and Gareth Bale with the goals. The Sandro-Dembele partnership was particularly impressive on an afternoon where the 3-1 score line didn't reflect the dominant performance. Two goals in 60 seconds changed everything as the team turned around a half-time deficit to topple QPR and secure a first win at White Hart Lane. QPR led through Bobby Zamora but an own goal and another from Jermain Defoe sealed the win. Our next fixture will live long in the memory of Spurs supporters, as we secured our first win at Old Trafford since 1989. Jonny Evans' own goal and a goal-of-the-season contender from Gareth Bale gave Spurs a 2-0 half-time lead. Nani pulled a goal back early in the second half. On 51 minutes Clint Dempsey scored a crucial third goal for Spurs. Shinji Kagawa immediately struck again for United as they poured forward, but we held on for a famous win. A great month for Tottenham Hotspur.

OCTOBER

Pld: 3 W: 2 D: 1 L: 0
End of month Position: 4th

Spurs continued to improve under Andre Villas-Boas. He seemed settled in his new role along with deadline-day signings Hugo Lloris and Clint Dempsey. New signings Mousa Dembele and Jan Vertonghen looked particularly impressive. Steven Caulker's first goal for the Club and one from Aaron Lennon gave Spurs all three points against Aston Villa. Chelsea were victorious at White Hart Lane in our next League match. Gary Cahill's volley put Chelsea ahead, but two goals in

quick succession from William Gallas and Jermain Defoe turned the game on its head. But Spurs, missing Gareth Bale and Mousa Dembele, couldn't hold on as goals from Juan Mata (2) and Daniel Sturridge sealed victory. We finished the month in the top four after a hard-fought victory at Southampton. Gareth Bale dispatched a clinical header from Tom Huddlestone's cross in the 15th minute and Clint Dempsey added a second. Jay Rodriguez pulled a goal back but we held on despite late pressure from Southampton.

NOVEMBER

Pld: 5 W: 2 D: 0 L: 3
End of month Position: 5th

Wigan's Ben Watson scored the only goal of the game in a match to forget at White Hart Lane. Despite late pressure, Roberto Martinez's side held on to earn a shock win. Edin Dzeko's late strike meant we left the Etihad empty-handed despite taking the lead through a Steven Caulker header. Sergio Aguero equalised for Manchester City before Dzeko's winner. We suffered a third successive defeat of the month at Arsenal, especially disappointing as we had the lead through Emmanuel Adebayor's early goal. But after he was sent off, it was one-way traffic. Gareth Bale scored our second goal, but Arsenal's man advantage was evident as they completed a 5-2 win. Another London derby was next on the fixture list as we produced a fine display to topple West Ham at the Lane. Jermain Defoe scored a terrific opener, Gareth Bale added a second before Defoe scored his second and Spurs' third. Andy Carroll pulled a goal back for West Ham. Three days later, the lads secured another three points after beating Liverpool in an entertaining game under the lights. Aaron Lennon put Spurs ahead, before Bale's sensational free-kick. An unfortunate Bale own goal gave Liverpool hope but we held on to earn three points.

DECEMBER

Pld: 6 W: 4 D: 1 L: 1
End of month Position: 3rd

Sandro's bolt from the blue and another double from Jermain Defoe secured a fine 3-0 win at Fulham. We were denied a fourth successive victory after Everton scored two stoppage-time goals at Goodison Park. Clint Dempsey's strike with 15 minutes remaining looked to be enough but we returned to London pointless. Jan Vertonghen's fantastic half volley was enough to see off an impressive Swansea side. Stoke were next to visit the Lane, but we were left frustrated as they held on to earn a point. It was a Boxing Day to remember as Gareth Bale led the way with a hat-trick as a dominant display yielded maximum points at Villa Park. Jermain Defoe scored the opening goal in one of the most one-sided Premier League away matches you'll see. A brilliant end to 2012 was complete with another away win. An own goal, and a superb piece of skill by Aaron Lennon was enough to move us up to third in the table with a 2-1 win at Sunderland.

JANUARY

Pld: 4 W: 1 D: 3 L: 0
End of month Position: 4th

Spurs remained third after coming from behind to beat Reading on New Year's Day. Michael Dawson levelled with a diving header from Gylfi Sigurdsson's corner. Emmanuel Adebayor put Spurs ahead and Clint Dempsey added a third to wrap up the win. We were held to a goalless draw at Queens Park Rangers, but the big disappointment was the knee injury Sandro suffered during the game. It was an injury that would keep him out for the rest of the season – a huge blow. Manchester United visited the Lane looking for revenge after our memorable win earlier in the season at Old Trafford. The game looked to be in serious doubt due to heavy snow, but it went ahead and it looked like United had done enough to win the match thanks to Robin van Persie's first-half header, but Clint Dempsey's stoppage-time goal earned a point, as we finally found a way past United in a dominant second-half performance. The Club secured another point, this time at Norwich, thanks to a superb solo effort from Gareth Bale. Lewis Holtby made his Spurs debut after signing from Schalke.

FEBRUARY

Pld: 3 W: 3 D: 0 L: 0
End of month Position: 3rd

Bale was on target again as we secured a hard-fought win over West Brom. It was also the Bale show as Newcastle visited the Lane. His first: a superb free-kick. Yoan Gouffran equalised midway through the half, but Bale scored the winner – his fourth goal in three League games. Bale's incredible February continued with two goals at West Ham. Andy Carroll and Joe Cole put West Ham ahead after Bale's opener, but a Gylfi Sigurdsson leveller and another goal-of-the-season contender from Bale secured a thrilling win at Upton Park.

MARCH

Pld: 4 W: 2 D: 0 L: 2
End of month Position: 3rd

Two goals in two first-half minutes paved the way for a magnificent derby day victory over Arsenal. Gareth Bale struck his 20th goal of the season in our colours and Aaron Lennon added a quick-fire second as we hit Arsenal with a double almost against the run of play in the first half, while the visitors' 51st-minute header from Per Mertesacker proved nothing more than a consolation. Our 12-game unbeaten run in the Premier League came to an end in a 3-2 reverse at Anfield as we suffered more Merseyside misery in an enthralling game. Two goals from Jan Vertonghen put Spurs in control, but goals from Suarez and Stewart Downing and a Steven Gerrard penalty put an end to our fine run. Our first home defeat since early November meant a disappointing afternoon at the Lane as former Spur Dimitar Berbatov's second-half strike was enough to earn Fulham a 1-0 win. Jan Vertonghen and Gareth Bale scored the goals as we secured the double over Swansea at the Liberty Stadium. Michu was on target for Swansea but Spurs held on.

APRIL

Pld: 3 W: 1 D: 2 L: 0
End of month Position: 5th

Gylfi Sigurdsson rescued a deserved point in a thrilling Premier League encounter against Everton at the Lane. Emmanuel Adebayor was also on target, opening the scoring inside the first minute. But Everton levelled through Phil Jagielka and took the lead from a fine solo goal by Kevin Mirallas. A draw was a fair result as both teams continued to chase Champions League football. Three goals in seven second-half minutes against Manchester City kept our top four hopes alive. Samir Nasri put City ahead, but Spurs won it with goals from Clint Dempsey, Jermain Defoe and Gareth Bale. Despite a stoppage time equaliser, it felt like two points dropped against Wigan at the DW Stadium. Gareth Bale put Spurs ahead but Emmerson Boyce and a stunning goal from Calum McManaman gave Wigan the lead. An own goal from Boyce earned a point.

MAY

Pld: 4 W: 3 D: 1 L: 0
Final Position: 5th

Southampton arrived at White Hart Lane full of confidence after beating Manchester City, Chelsea and Liverpool, and it took something special from Gareth Bale to win the game and he did so with a spectacular goal on 86 minutes. Spurs came from behind twice to earn a draw against Chelsea at Stamford Bridge. A brilliant solo goal from Emmanuel Adebayor and a goal from Gylfi Sigurdsson 10 minutes from full time earned a deserved point. Spurs had to win at Stoke as the battle for fourth place went down to the wire. Clint Dempsey levelled Steven Nzonzi's third-minute header with a fine strike in the 20th minute – firing into an empty net from 35 yards – and after dominating possession following Charlie Adam's sending off at the start of the second half, Adebayor clinched the win seven minutes from time. It was fitting to end the season with an outstanding goal from Gareth Bale. His stoppage-time winner against Sunderland wasn't enough to secure Champions League football. We finished in fifth with a Club record Premier League haul of 72 points.

FINAL PREMIER LEAGUE TABLE

POS	CLUB	P	W	D	L	GF	GA	GD	PTS
1	Manchester United	38	28	5	5	86	43	43	89
2	Manchester City	38	23	9	6	66	34	32	78
3	Chelsea	38	22	9	7	75	39	36	75
4	Arsenal	38	21	10	7	72	37	35	73
5	Tottenham Hotspur	38	21	9	8	66	46	20	72
6	Everton	38	16	15	7	55	40	15	63
7	Liverpool	38	16	13	9	71	43	28	61
8	West Bromwich Albion	38	14	7	17	53	57	-4	49
9	Swansea City	38	11	13	14	47	51	-4	46
10	West Ham United	38	12	10	16	45	53	-8	46
11	Norwich City	38	10	14	14	41	58	-17	44
12	Fulham	38	11	10	17	50	60	-10	43
13	Stoke City	38	9	15	14	34	45	-11	42
14	Southampton	38	9	14	15	49	60	-11	41
15	Aston Villa	38	10	11	17	47	69	-22	41
16	Newcastle United	38	11	8	19	45	68	-23	41
17	Sunderland	38	9	12	17	41	54	-13	39
18	Wigan Athletic	38	9	9	20	47	73	-26	36
19	Reading	38	6	10	22	43	73	-30	28
20	Queens Park Rangers	38	4	13	21	30	60	-30	25

UEFA EUROPA LEAGUE REVIEW

There were plenty of memorable moments during the UEFA Europa League campaign, including a superb 3-0 victory against Inter Milan at White Hart Lane. Head Coach Andre Villas-Boas has made no secret of his desire to lift this trophy again. Fingers crossed, 2014 will be the year it returns to White Hart Lane!

UEFA EUROPA LEAGUE GROUP J

Tottenham Hotspur 0-0 Lazio

Our opening match in the Europa League ended goalless against high-flying Lazio. We had three goals disallowed – Clint Dempsey in the first half, Jermain Defoe and Steven Caulker in the second – and dominated the majority of possession without reward. Hugo Lloris made his Spurs debut.

Lloris, Walker, Caulker, Vertonghen, Naughton, Sandro, Dembele (Mason 90), Dempsey (Sigurdsson 76), Lennon (Townsend 81), Bale, Defoe

Panathinaikos 1-1 Tottenham Hotspur

Spurs dominated this match, but Toche's late strike denied us maximum points. Michael Dawson put Spurs ahead after glancing home Tom Huddlestone's free-kick.

Lloris, Walker, Caulker, Dawson, Vertonghen, Huddlestone (Sandro 81), Dembele, Dempsey (Sigurdsson 66), Lennon (Townsend 75), Bale, Defoe

Maribor 1-1 Tottenham Hotspur

Gylfi Sigurdsson scored to earn a point for Spurs. It was our third straight draw which left us third in the group. Aaron Lennon was named captain.

Lloris, Naughton, Vertonghen, Caulker, Walker, Huddlestone, Lennon, Sigurdsson (Dempsey 75), Sandro (Livermore 84), Townsend (Falque 46), Defoe

Tottenham Hotspur 3-1 Maribor

A hat-trick from Jermain Defoe sealed all three points for Spurs who dominated from the first to the last minute, with Tom Carroll impressing the White Hart Lane crowd in central midfield.

Lloris, Walker, Dawson, Vertonghen, Naughton, Huddlestone, Lennon (Falque 90), Bale (Mason 86), Carroll, Adebayor, Defoe

Lazio 0-0 Tottenham Hotspur

A fine defensive display led by Hugo Lloris secured a point against Lazio. This meant Spurs only needed a draw at home to Panathinaikos to secure a place in the round of 32.

Lloris, Walker, Caulker, Vertonghen, Naughton, Sigurdsson (Lennon 63), Sandro, Carroll (Dembele 76), Bale, Dempsey (Defoe 63), Adebayor

Tottenham Hotspur 3-1 Panathinaikos

Spurs secured their place in the round of 32 after beating Panathinaikos. Emmanuel Adebayor put Spurs ahead after 29 minutes. Zeca levelled for the Greek side on 54 minutes. Keeper Orestis Karnezis directed Clint Dempsey's header into his own goal to put Spurs ahead and Jermain Defoe secured the win with a clever dink on 83 minutes. Andre Villas-Boas made no secret of his desire to go all the way in the competition and the players were responding to his ambition.

Friedel, Walker, Caulker, Vertonghen, Naughton, Lennon (Livermore 87), Sandro, Carroll (Dembele 75), Dempsey (Sigurdsson 80), Adebayor, Defoe

UEFA EUROPA LEAGUE LAST 32 FIRST LEG

Tottenham Hotspur 2-1 Lyon

Not for the first time in the campaign, this was the Gareth Bale show. The Welsh international scored a superb free-kick in first-half stoppage-time against a very talented Lyon side. The French side levelled with a technically perfect half-volley from the edge of the box to level the game. But in stoppage-time, Bale stepped up again and scored yet another unstoppable free-kick. An entertaining game full of stunning goals.

Friedel, Walker, Gallas, Vertonghen, Assou-Ekotto, Lennon (Sigurdsson 79), Dembele, Parker (Livermore 90), Dempsey (Holtby 67), Bale, Adebayor

UEFA EUROPA LEAGUE LAST 32 SECOND LEG

Lyon 1-1 Tottenham Hotspur (Tottenham Hotspur win 3-2 on aggregate)

Mousa Dembele's wonder strike in the final minute secured a 1-1 draw on the night and a 3-2 win on aggregate. Spurs looked to be heading out before Dembele picked up the ball 30 yards from goal, shifted away from Maxime Gonalons and fired into the corner from 25 yards.

Friedel, Walker, Gallas, Vertonghen, Assou-Ekotto, Lennon (Dempsey 66), Dembele, Parker (Livermore 84), Holtby (Sigurdsson 74), Bale, Adebayor

UEFA EUROPA LEAGUE LAST 16 FIRST LEG

Tottenham Hotspur 3-0 Inter Milan

Gareth Bale was the star of the show once again as Spurs totally dominated Inter Milan at White Hart Lane. Bale glanced in a header from Gylfi Sigurdsson's cross early on, then it was Sigurdsson's turn to get on the score sheet. Jan Vertonghen headed in a third from Bale's corner in the second half to give Spurs a strong advantage.

Friedel, Walker, Gallas, Vertonghen, Assou-Ekotto, Lennon (Naughton 81), Dembele (Livermore 64), Parker, Sigurdsson, Bale, Defoe

UEFA EUROPA LEAGUE LAST 16 SECOND LEG

Inter Milan 4-1 Tottenham Hotspur (After extra-time, Tottenham Hotspur win on away goals)

Emmanuel Adebayor scored a crucial extra-time away goal to seal our place in the quarter-final. Inter overturned a three-goal deficit from the first leg as Antonio Cassano headed in before Rodrigo Palacio's finish and a William Gallas own goal drew the tie level. The away goal arrived on 96 minutes when Adebayor slid in the rebound after Samir

Handanovic palmed out Mousa Dembele's drive. Ricardo Alvarez put Inter 4-1 ahead but we held on despite a great comeback from the Italian giants.

Friedel, Walker, Gallas, Vertonghen, Naughton (Caulker 104), Parker (Naughton 81), Livermore (Lennon 70), Sigurdsson, Dembele, Defoe (Holtby 56), Adebayor

UEFA EUROPA LEAGUE QUARTER-FINAL FIRST LEG

Tottenham Hotspur 2-2 FC Basel

The team fought back from 2-0 down to keep our Europa League quarter-final alive against an impressive FC Basel side. The Swiss champions took a grip of the game in the first half with two goals in quick succession from Valentin Stocker and Fabian Frei. Spurs hit back through Emmanuel Adebayor five minutes before half time and levelled in the 57th minute when Gylfi Sigurdsson let fly from 20 yards. The match ended on a sour note as Gareth Bale limped off with an ankle injury which would keep him out of the return leg.

Friedel, Naughton, Gallas, Vertonghen, Assou-Ekotto (Dawson 57), Lennon (Sigurdsson 24), Parker, Bale, Holtby (Dempsey 63), Dembele, Adebayor

UEFA EUROPA LEAGUE QUARTER-FINAL SECOND LEG

FC Basel 2-2 Tottenham Hotspur (After extra-time, FC Basel win 4-1 on penalties)

Our Europa League adventure came to an end after a 4-1 defeat on penalties. Clint Dempsey put Spurs ahead on 23 minutes. The home side levelled through Mohamed Salah. Aleksandar Dragovic made it 2-1 from close range after we failed to clear a corner, before Dempsey levelled, while Jan Vertonghen was sent off close to the end of normal time. After extra time Tom Huddlestone and Emmanuel Adebayor missed their penalties to send Basel through. A heartbreaking end after an exciting run in the competition.

Friedel, Walker, Dawson, Vertonghen, Naughton (Assou-Ekotto 78), Sigurdsson, Parker (Huddlestone 77), Dembele (Carroll 59), Holtby, Dempsey, Adebayor

DOMESTIC CUPS
REVIEW

FA CUP THIRD ROUND

TOTTENHAM HOTSPUR 3-0 COVENTRY CITY

Clint Dempsey scored twice as we comfortably beat League One Coventry in front of a sold-out White Hart Lane. Dempsey opened the scoring on 14 minutes, after getting the final touch from a free-kick. Gareth Bale scored the second on 33 minutes after converting from close range. Dempsey's second of the afternoon came on 37 minutes. Thankfully no repeat of the 1987 final.

Friedel, Naughton, Dawson, Assou-Ekotto, Caulker, Dempsey, Huddlestone, Parker (Dembele 80), Bale (Townsend 70), Sigurdsson (Carroll 79), Adebayor

FA CUP FOURTH ROUND

LEEDS UNITED 2-1 TOTTENHAM HOTSPUR

Our FA Cup run came to an end after a disappointing defeat at Elland Road. Luke Varney put the Championship side ahead on 15 minutes. Ross McCormack made it 2-0 on 50 minutes. Clint Dempsey pulled a goal back eight minutes later, but Leeds held on.

Friedel, Naughton (Walker 66), Vertonghen, Caulker, Assou-Ekotto , Parker, Huddlestone (Dembele 59), Lennon, Dempsey, Bale, Sigurdsson (Obika 59)

CAPITAL ONE CUP THIRD ROUND

CARLISLE 0-3 TOTTENHAM HOTSPUR

Jan Vertonghen scored his first goal for Spurs in a comfortable win. Andros Townsend put Spurs in control with a brilliant solo effort on 53 minutes. Gylfi Sigurdsson was also on target. Youngsters Ryan Mason, Adam Smith and Yago Falque all started the match.

Cudicini, Smith, Vertonghen (Walker 65), Dawson, Caulker, Dempsey (Obika 75), Huddlestone, Sigurdsson, Falque, Townsend, Mason (Carroll 70)

CAPITAL ONE CUP FOURTH ROUND

NORWICH 2-1 TOTTENHAM HOTSPUR

Norwich produced a late comeback as we bowed out of the Capital One Cup at Carrow Road. Spurs were on top throughout the match, so it was no surprise to see Gareth Bale give Spurs the lead on 66 minutes. A deflected Alex Tettey shot for Norwich meant the tie was going into extra-time, but Simeon Jackson's late goal earned victory for Chris Hughton's side. Clint Dempsey saw his stoppage-time penalty saved by Mark Bunn.

Lloris, Walker (Defoe 90), Dawson, Caulker, Naughton, Sigurdsson, Falque, Livermore (Huddlestone 46), Carroll (Vertonghen 79), Dempsey, Bale

HUGO LLORIS

It didn't take long for Hugo Lloris to become a crowd favourite at White Hart Lane. The French captain caught the eye with commanding displays throughout his debut Barclays Premier League season.

Supporters were impressed with lightning reflexes off his line and excellent decision-making. Hugo also proved to be a difficult opponent to beat in one-on-one situations.

The 26-year-old became an essential part of our pressing game, almost operating as a sweeper behind the two central defenders, allowing us to play an advanced line.

After his first full season in England, Hugo already has a strong bond with his current club.

"I really appreciate playing for Tottenham, playing at White Hart Lane with great fans. The fans travel with us everywhere. I think there is a big community in White Hart Lane between players and fans."

Despite the disappointment of finishing outside the top four, Hugo was quick to point out many great performances from the side last season.

"We won a lot of important games last season against teams like Arsenal and Manchester City; that was when we really felt the power of our fans. It was a great feeling. I had a lot of great moments from my first season and I hope to have a lot of great moments in the future and I hope to win trophies with Tottenham Hotspur. That's important for the Club, the players and for the supporters."

Hugo had to wait until October last season to cement his place as our number one. Brad Friedel was hard to dislodge, but after impressing in the UEFA Europa League, Hugo was given his full League debut against Aston Villa at White Hart Lane.

Lloris kept us in the match with a string of superb saves during his debut against Lazio, the 1-0 victory at home to Southampton and in the 3-1 win against Manchester City where he thwarted Carlos Tevez-and-co time and time again.

But Hugo's save against West Ham at Upton Park stands out. With the Hammers leading 2-1, the Frenchman raced off his line to make a brilliant stop against Matt Taylor which kept us in the match.

We like our goalkeepers at Spurs. Pat Jennings, Ray Clemence and Paul Robinson will tell you that, and only after one season, it looks like Hugo will be joining that elite group.

KEY STATS
(Premier League)

Games:	27
Saves:	51
Goals against:	29
Clean sheets:	9

ANDRE VILLAS-BOAS

After an impressive first season at Tottenham Hotspur, Andre Villas-Boas is looking forward to an even better campaign than last year.

Andre was given the task of handling a transitional period at the Club, which included the exciting move to the new training ground in Enfield. There were also big changes on the playing side, with Luka Modric and Rafa van der Vaart departing. Ledley King had also announced his retirement. Injuries to Younes Kaboul, Benoit Assou-Ekotto and Scott Parker didn't help as the side struggled in its opening three League matches.

After a difficult start, the new arrivals settled well and the new Head Coach's training methods began to be implemented. Impressive results followed including a memorable 3-2 win against Manchester United at Old Trafford.

Andre's attention to detail didn't go unnoticed with the players. The Club were often criticised for leaking late goals, but, under

Andre, 23 points were won from losing positions. Much credit for that should go to the Head Coach.

With seven top class internationals joining the Club since last season, Villas-Boas now has a squad capable of playing his preferred 4-3-3 system. His central midfielders should have strong attributes in pace, power and an ability to attack and defend. Summer signings Etienne Capoue and Paulinho are both ideal for this role. For Andre, wingers should be comfortable on both feet, with a tendency to cut inside and unleash a shot from outside the area. Nacer Chadli and Erik Lamela have both settled into this system well and with Andre's emphasis on hard work in training, the future looks promising for Spurs.

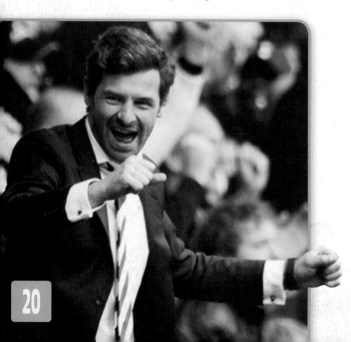

"All the lads love him. He's got great ideas. He's really organised."
– Jermain Defoe

PLAYER PROFILES

HUGO LLORIS

Hugo enjoyed a successful first season at White Hart Lane. The France captain joined from Lyon on 31 August 2012. Hugo made 146 League appearances for Lyon, twice winning the Ligue 1 Goalkeeper of the Year award.

BRAD FRIEDEL

Holder of the record for consecutive starts in the Premier League. Brad is now in his third season at the Club. At 42, Brad is still part of the First Team squad used primarily for cup competitions.

YOUNES KABOUL

The French international made only one appearance last season due to a serious knee injury. Now fully fit, Younes is considered one of the best centre-backs in the Premier League.

JAN VERTONGHEN

Jan made a huge impression in his first season at the Club. The central defender scored an impressive eight goals, including a goal-of-the-season contender against Swansea. Jan is also accomplished at left-back. The Belgium international is a key member of the first team.

KYLE NAUGHTON

Kyle made 14 appearances for Spurs last season. The former England Under-21 international was used primarily at left-back last season and his versatility was important as we continued to combine our League campaign with the Europa League.

MICHAEL DAWSON

Michael is now in his 10th season at the Club. The popular defender is the current Club captain. The England international started his career at Nottingham Forest before joining the Club in 2004. Dawson was named our 'Player of the Year' in 2009/2010.

DANNY ROSE

Danny enjoyed a hugely successful spell at Sunderland last season. This quick, aggressive left-sided player has developed into a fine left-back after starting out at Spurs as a left winger.

KYLE WALKER

The England international is now in his fifth season at the Club. Kyle was named PFA Young Player of the Year in 2011/2012. The right-back made 47 appearances for Spurs last season.

PLAYER PROFILES

VLAD CHIRICHES

Vlad became the fifth player to join Spurs in the summer. The 23-year old made a total of 62 appearances for Steaua Bucharest, scoring four times, and his impressive appearances at club level have seen him capped on 19 occasions so far by the Romania national team.

AARON LENNON

Aaron is now in his ninth season at the Club. The winger made 48 appearances last season, scoring the second goal in the North London derby. Aaron is capable of winning any match with a turn of pace down either flank.

ETIENNE CAPOUE

The French international midfielder joined us from Toulouse in August, 2013. Capoue, 25, made 174 appearances, scoring 13 times in Ligue 1 for Toulouse and was named in the League's Team of the Year in 2012 alongside Hugo Lloris.

LEWIS HOLTBY

Lewis joined the Club from Schalke in January, 2013. The German international featured in the European Under-21 Championships in Israel last summer. Lewis made 160 appearances in his career in Germany, scoring 29 times.

MOUSA DEMBELE

The Belgium international made 40 appearances in an impressive first season at White Hart Lane. Tough in the tackle, an eye for a pass, Mousa will undoubtedly feature heavily in the first team throughout the season.

SANDRO

A real character, Sandro is full of energy on and off the field! It was a huge loss to the team when he suffered a serious knee injury against Queens Park Rangers in January, 2013. A key member of the Brazilian national team, Sandro is also an Olympic silver medallist.

ANDROS TOWNSEND

Andros impressed during his loan spell at Queens Park Rangers last season. The Under-21 international scored two goals during his spell at Loftus Road. The winger will be an important part of the squad in a busy season.

NACER CHADLI

The Belgium international joined Spurs from FC Twente in July. After joining FC Twente from AGOVV Apeldoorn in 2010, he went on to make 106 appearances for the Dutch side, scoring 31 goals.

PLAYER PROFILES

PAULINHO

Brazilian international midfielder Paulinho joined us from Corinthians in July 2013. The 24-year-old, capped by Brazil 17 times, helped his country to FIFA Confederations Cup success in July 2013 with victory against world champions Spain, and also scored the equaliser against England in the 2-2 draw at the Maracana last month.

GYLFI SIGURDSSON

Gylfi scored seven goals last season. The popular Icelandic international is comfortable in a variety of positions but found himself on the wing due to Gareth Bale's form, just behind the lone striker.

ERIK LAMELA

Erik became the sixth player to join Spurs in the summer. The 21-year old attacking midfielder came through the ranks at River Plate and went on to make 40 appearances before joining Roma in 2011, where he made a total of 67 appearances in all competitions and scored 21 goals.

CHRISTIAN ERIKSEN

Christian joined Spurs from Ajax. The Denmark international moved to Ajax in 2008 from Odense in his homeland and has since gone on to play a total of 161 games for the Eredivisie club, scoring 33 times.

JERMAIN DEFOE

The England international is now in his 11th season at the Club. The popular striker scored 15 goals for Spurs last season. Defoe's goal against Manchester City in April moved him up to seventh in Spurs' all-time scoring record.

EMMANUEL ADEBAYOR

Emmanuel scored eight goals last season. The Togo international scored one of the goals of the season against Chelsea. 'Ade' has also played for Arsenal, Real Madrid and Manchester City before signing for Spurs.

ROBERTO SOLDADO

The Spanish international joined the Club from Valencia for a Club-record fee in August 2013. Roberto scored 80 times in 146 appearances during his time at the Mestalla which he joined from Getafe in 2010, after impressing with a tally of 29 goals in 60 League appearances.

GYLFI SIGURDSSON

DANNY ROSE

ROBERTO SOLDADO

Roberto Soldado joined Tottenham Hotspur for a Club-record fee in August. The Spain international arrived in North London after three successful years at Valencia.

It was a busy summer at White Hart Lane with a number of arrivals, but Soldado, our new number 9, was particularly eye-catching. Roberto, who represented Spain at all youth levels, is now a regular in Vicente del Bosque's side. He scored 80 goals in 145 games for Valencia and is determined to replicate his goal-scoring in England. "I've come here as a striker to score goals. I always try to achieve more goals in the next season, so that will be my aim, to score as many goals as I can for Spurs next season."

Soldado also had a very impressive record in the UEFA Champions League, scoring 16 goals in 25 matches. The 28 year-old is now relishing the challenge of helping his new side into the top four. "Spurs is a great club and a club that deserves to be in the Champions League. I know it's a hard league and we have to work and play to that level to get there and I will do my best for the team."

The 28 year-old began his career at Real Madrid, where he scored 63 goals in 120 League appearances for the B side, Real Madrid Castilla, also featuring on 16 occasions for the First Team either side of a loan move to Osasuna in season 2006/2007, when he scored 11 goals in 30 appearances before moving to Getafe in 2008.

The Spain international now has 11 caps to his name and has scored six goals for his country, with his most recent appearances coming in the Confederations Cup, staged in Brazil in June.

"I love playing in a team like that, a team that holds onto the ball and then attacks. It's Andre's style and it's good for the fans to see that (style of) football and for the team as well."

Roberto scored on his debut as Spurs beat Crystal Palace 1-0 on the opening day of the season. Soldado also scored a penalty against Espanyol at White Hart Lane in pre-season, and was cool and clinical in his execution.

The fans were certainly delighted with the capture of Soldado, and his popularity is reflected in the large number choosing to have 'Soldado 9' printed on the back of their shirts. Lineker, Sheringham, Klinsmann, van der Vaart and Keane were hugely popular forwards at the Lane. And, after Soldado's encouraging start, his popularity is likely to emulate former Spurs heroes.

"I'm absolutely honoured to be at this club. To wear the shirt that has so much history"

JAN
VERTONGHEN

Jan Vertonghen's performances in his first season in England show Tottenham Hotspur are well covered in defence.

The tall Belgian came to England with a big reputation after being voted the player of the year in Holland, having had a fantastic season with Ajax, and now that reputation has spread across Europe after a brilliant first season in the Premier League.

An intelligent footballer who reads the game brilliantly, Jan added another dimension to our game with his ability to drive the ball forward out from the defence. His powering run from left back, which resulted in a goal at Manchester United was just one early sign Spurs could rely on Jan to produce goals from the back. Further strikes against Swansea and Liverpool confirmed his goalscoring threat.

In March 2013, Jan was named Barclay's Player of the Month for his consistently excellent performances. More accolades followed, notably his inclusion in the PFA Team of the Year.

JAN'S GREAT GOALS 2012/2013

SWANSEA (A)

Vertonghen carried the ball out of defence and slid it to Gareth Bale, continued his run forward collecting Bale's return in the box, controlled it and touched home past Michel Vorm.

LIVERPOOL (A)

Jan's second goal of the afternoon came after a Bale free-kick was lofted into the box. Neither Michael Dawson or Glen Johnson could make contact and it bounced off Daniel Agger into the path of Vertonghen, whose right-footed half volley beat Brad Jones and nestled in the back of the net.

KEY STATS (PREMIER LEAGUE)	
Games	34
Goals	4
Assists	4
Goals against	41

ETIENNE CAPOUE

Etienne became our fourth summer signing after joining the Club from French side Toulouse. The France international, at age 25, has made 174 appearances, scoring 13 times in Ligue 1 for Toulouse, and was named in the League's Team of the Year in 2012 alongside Hugo Lloris.

The powerful defensive midfielder, who can also be employed at centre-half, has represented his country at Under-18, 19 and 21 levels, and is now a regular in the full international squad.

Etienne made his Spurs debut against Crystal Palace, replacing Mousa Dembele early in the second half, and impressed immediately. Holding onto a 1-0 lead, Etienne made crucial interceptions, solid passing and lung-busting runs to help earn three points on the opening day.

"It's a very big club. I'm happy to be here. There is a great spirit within the squad – I like the atmosphere."

"I saw a lot of Tottenham last season. I like the way they played. It's a style that suits me. I am pleased I am here. The Premier League is where I wanted to be. I want to play as much as I can in the League and in Europe."

As supporters have already witnessed, Etienne can start attacks with defence-splitting passes, plus he has an ability to shoot with power after venturing forward, dispossessing opposition players along the way.

A successful season for Etienne and Spurs is likely to see him included in the France squad for the 2014 World Cup in Brazil, where he will join team-mate and national captain Hugo Lloris.

"Hugo is an amazing goalkeeper. He told me Tottenham was a good club to join. They always fight to finish in the top four and that's the aim again this season."

TOTTENHAM HOTSPUR
ALL-TIME GREATS

Can you find the names of TEN Spurs legends in this word search?
Words can go horizontally, vertically and diagonally.

```
Y  H  R  K  T  P  M  B  D  B  K  Y
L  V  E  I  N  R  G  B  N  L  R  O
L  G  W  N  R  A  T  I  I  L  D  P
R  N  O  G  F  W  M  N  N  A  T  E
S  X  L  X  C  K  S  Y  D  O  L  Z
E  D  F  F  L  M  X  L  R  D  L  T
L  L  H  Q  A  T  O  K  D  R  Z  A
I  B  C  N  Z  S  D  O  P  M  E  C
D  Y  N  B  C  P  H  F  H  N  K  P
R  B  A  G  A  S  C  O  I  G  N  E
A  M  L  Q  G  Q  Y  N  K  P  X  N
K  B  B  L  T  T  U  B  B  A  M  D
```

Ardiles	King	Soldado
Klinsmann	Blanchflower	Mabbutt
Perryman	Ginola	Hoddle
		Gascoigne

ANSWERS ON PAGE 60

35

PAULINHO

The Brazilian international joined Tottenham Hotspur in July 2013 after a successful Confederations Cup campaign with Brazil.

The box-to-box midfielder was named third best player at the tournament after a number of impressive performances. Despite interest from around Europe, Paulinho decided to join Tottenham Hotspur and link up with fellow Brazilians Heurelho Gomes and Sandro.

Paulinho has enjoyed great success since joining the Corinthians from Brazilian Serie B side Clube Atlético Bragantino in 2010. He made a total of 86 League appearances, scoring 20 goals while helping the Sao Paulo-based club to the Brazilian Serie A League Championship in 2011 as well as the Copa Libertadores and FIFA Club World Cup a year later. His performances at club level have also seen him twice named in the Serie A Team of the Year in 2011 and 2012.

The 24-year-old, capped by Brazil 17 times, was involved in the Confederations Cup victory against world champions Spain and also scored the equaliser against England in the 2-2 draw at the Maracana.

"I am very happy and excited to have joined Spurs. It's a huge pleasure for my career to be at a club as big as Tottenham. I know it will be a huge challenge but I think I can help all my colleagues to succeed and give a lot of happiness to the supporters.

"The Training Centre is amazing and I'm very impressed about the conditions Tottenham offers to the players. I will focus on my job and use the facility as much as possible."

Paulinho has already made a big impact on the Spurs supporters and looks comfortable at the heart of the mouth-watering midfield alongside Sandro and Mousa Dembele.

"We used to watch the Premier League in Brazil – including Tottenham – and this Club has big players. I just want to help them to succeed here. It's nice to have another Brazilian in the squad and I'm excited to work with Sandro and all the players."

NACER CHADLI

Nacer became our second summer signing, arriving shortly after Brazilian international Paulinho. The Belgian international can play anywhere behind the lone striker, which makes him a perfect addition to Andre Villas-Boas' side.

Chadli is an important part of a Belgium side that has a genuine chance of World Cup glory in the summer. The 25-year-old spent three successful years at FC Twente, scoring twice against Spurs in the UEFA Champions League in 2010. He scored once at White Hart Lane, but Spurs won 4-1. His second goal came in a December match – a superb free-kick in an entertaining 3-3 draw.

Nacer immediately felt at home in North London, and it certainly helped having his Belgium team-mates Jan Vertonghen and Mousa Dembele already at the Club. Tottenham Hotspur was just one of a number of clubs interested in Nacer in the summer, but he told us there was only one club he wanted to join.

"I'm happy that Jan and Mousa are already here, they helped me a lot in the summer. All the guys are nice guys, so that's made it easier for me to come into the group."

"It was always a dream for me to play in the Premier League and to play for the right club. Some clubs wanted me this summer but Tottenham Hotspur was the best choice for me and the best club. I played here three years ago for Twente and I was really impressed with the Club, the stadium and all the players."

Nacer's versatility will be crucial as Spurs contest four competitions. The winger scored an impressive 31 goals in 106 matches, and he's determined to sustain that record at his new Club.

"On the wings you normally give more assists, but I scored more goals. It's important to try and improve every game, to make an assist or a goal to help the team win."

37

You're the star!

SPURS JUNIOR MEMBERSHIP IS NOW OUR BEST EVER

LOOK AT ALL THESE GREAT REASONS TO JOIN US AS A JUNIOR MEMBER

- Exclusive **GOODIE** packs
- **TICKET** priority and discounts
- **FREE** STADIUM TOUR (worth £9)
- **NEW!** Chance to become a MATCHDAY FLAGWAVER
- **WIN** invitations to Christmas party with players
- Chance to **STAR** in the new squad photo
- **NEW!** Free chances to PLAY ON THE PITCH (worth £70)
- **NEW!** FREE SOCCER SCHOOLS PLACES and meet the players
- Chance to **INTERVIEW** a player
- Chance to present Player of the Season **TROPHY**
- Birthday and Christmas **CARDS**
- Junior **MAGAZINES**

EXCLUSIVE TO JUNIOR MEMBERS

BE A PART OF THE TEAM!
JOIN US TODAY AS A ONE HOTSPUR JUNIOR MEMBER:

01 **Visit** tottenhamhotspur.com/juniors
02 **Call: 0844 8440102 Option 2**

MEET THE STAFF

Andre Villas-Boas' coaching team

ASSISTANT HEAD COACH
STEFFEN FREUND

This Spurs legend needs no introduction. Steffen returned to Spurs as Assistant Head Coach to Andre Villas-Boas in July 2012.

Steffen is a Hall of Fame inductee and played for Spurs from 1999-2003. After retiring, Steffen embarked on a coaching career which has included spells as co-trainer of the Germany Under-20 squad, assistant manager of the Nigerian national team for their African Cup of Nations campaign in 2007-2008; and head coach of the German Under-16 team.

FIRST TEAM FITNESS COACH JOSE MARIO ROCHA

Arrived at White Hart Lane with Andre Villas-Boas, having worked alongside our new Head Coach throughout his management career so far. Jose has 19 years of experience working in the professional game, the first 17 of those in the set-up at Porto where he was employed as a general coach.

FIRST TEAM COACH
LUIS MARTINS

Appointed to the role of First Team Coach having first embarked on a coaching career with hometown club Sporting Lisbon.

Born in the Portuguese capital Lisbon on November 29, 1963, it was as a coach that he made his name, taking charge of Sporting's youth teams and winning national titles as coach of their Under-17 and Under-19 sides in 2004 and 2006 respectively, working with teams which included Cristiano Ronaldo, Nani and Joao Moutinho.

GOALKEEPING COACH
TONY PARKS

A true Spurs legend. Parks saved the penalty to win the 1984 UEFA Cup. Tony returned to the Club as goalkeeping coach in November 2008, having spent the previous six years working in a similar role with the FA, coaching the England youth teams.

HEAD OF OPPOSITION SCOUTING
DANIEL SOUSA

A knee injury ended Daniel's playing career. Retirement led to him studying sports science. He followed Andre Villas-Boas to Porto and Chelsea, working in the field of opposition scouting and providing the coaches with information to help plot the downfall of opponents.

LADS TRAINING

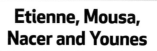

Etienne, Mousa, Nacer and Younes

On your marks, Zeki!

Andros, before his man-of-the-match performance against Dinamo Tbilisi

Andre keeps his
eye on the ball!

Mousa in the middle!

INTERNATIONAL SPURS

International weekend on Hotspur Way can be a quiet time with many of the team away playing for their country. As you can see, Tottenham Hotspur have many international players from all over the world.

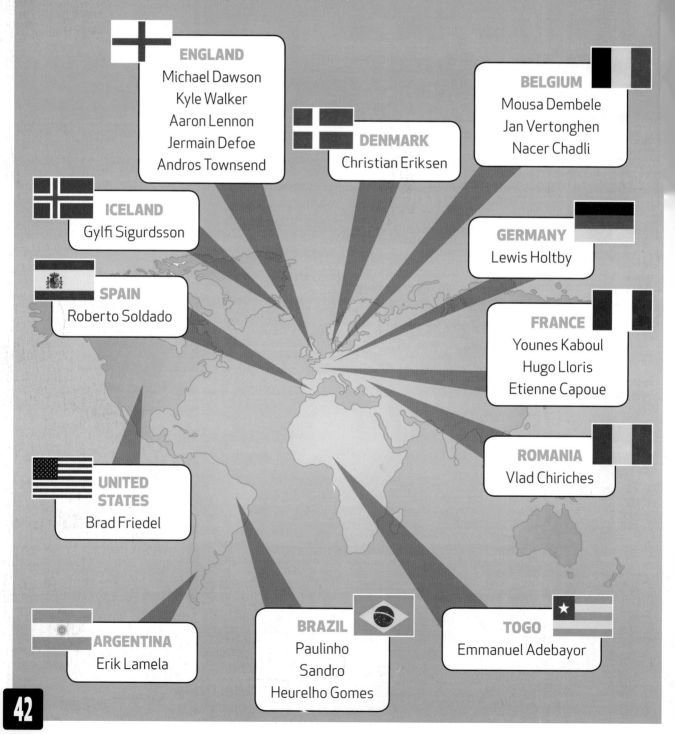

ENGLAND
Michael Dawson
Kyle Walker
Aaron Lennon
Jermain Defoe
Andros Townsend

DENMARK
Christian Eriksen

BELGIUM
Mousa Dembele
Jan Vertonghen
Nacer Chadli

ICELAND
Gylfi Sigurdsson

GERMANY
Lewis Holtby

SPAIN
Roberto Soldado

FRANCE
Younes Kaboul
Hugo Lloris
Etienne Capoue

ROMANIA
Vlad Chiriches

UNITED STATES
Brad Friedel

ARGENTINA
Erik Lamela

BRAZIL
Paulinho
Sandro
Heurelho Gomes

TOGO
Emmanuel Adebayor

HOTSPUR WAY

The Tottenham Hotspur Training Centre has been built on 77 acres and is located on Hotspur Way, Enfield. It is the home of the Club's First Team and Academy and is recognised as one of the best in Europe.

The state-of-the-art facility — which includes a covered artificial pitch, world-class player preparation areas, pool and hydrotherapy complex, altitude room, large-scale gymnasium and specialist sports rehabilitation suites — will support the Club's ambitions to attract, develop and retain the highest quality talent.

SPURS LEGENDS

Do you want to know why Tottenham Hotspur is such a special Club? Spurs has always attracted world class talent. Some have become White Hart Lane legends. In a new yearly feature, you can remember them here.

Jimmy Greaves

JIMMY GREAVES

Spurs signed Jimmy for £99,999, as manager Bill Nicholson did not want him to become burdened by being the first £100,000 footballer. He continued to set goalscoring records in North London and for three successive seasons was the leading First Division striker. He scored after just three minutes as Spurs won the FA Cup in 1962 and netted two against Athletic Madrid in the final of the 1963 Cup Winners' Cup. Jimmy first played for England in 1959, scoring 44 goals in 57 games. The six hat-tricks he scored still stand as an England record. Jimmy is Tottenham Hotspur's all-time leading goal scorer with 266 goals in 379 games in all competitions.

JURGEN KLINSMANN

Jurgen took only 18 months to become a legend at White Hart Lane. Few will forget the impact the German star made in 1994/1995 when he scored 29 goals in that campaign as we overcame the mid-season departure of Ossie Ardiles to finish seventh in the Premiership and reach the semi-finals of the FA Cup under Gerry Francis. After a successful time with Bayern Munich, Klinsmann returned for his second spell from Sampdoria in December 1997. It was a different scenario this time, with us fighting relegation under the leadership of Christian Gross. Klinsmann scored four goals in a key 6-2 win at Wimbledon in the season's penultimate game. Klinsmann signed off with a cracker against Southampton on the final day – it would be his last Club game. He retired after representing Germany in the World Cup that summer.

Jurgen Klinsmann

Dave Mackay

RICKY VILLA

Ricky's move to White Hart Lane shocked the football world. Villa joined with Argentina team-mate Ossie Ardiles after the 1978 World Cup. Ricky was the man for the big occasions. He scored a hat-trick on the day the new West Stand was opened at White Hart Lane in a 6-1 win over Wolves in February 1982. But his greatest Spurs memory was in the FA Cup final replay in 1981. The Argentine seemed to have the ball glued to his feet as he tricked his way past the Manchester City defenders to slot home the winner. A Tottenham Hotspur legend was born and Spurs defeated Manchester City 3-2 to win the 1981 FA Cup.

DAVE MACKAY

Described by Bill Nicholson as his best signing, Dave Mackay was the heartbeat of the Double-winning side and one of the Club's greatest players. Famed for his tough tackling, stamina, enthusiasm and never-say-die attitude, Mackay was a magnificent all-round player with superb skills, passing and an eye for goal. After 10 years at the Lane he was granted a transfer to Derby County who he helped to the Second Division title and was named joint Football Writers' Player of the Year.

Ricky Villa

Pat Jennings

PAT JENNINGS

Pat Jennings will be remembered as one of the finest goalkeepers to ever grace the game. 'Big Pat' played 673 games for Spurs between 1964 and 1977 and another 300-plus at Arsenal before winding down his career in a second spell at White Hart Lane. He also played 119 times for Northern Ireland, including two World Cups. After retirement, Pat has spent over 10 years as goalkeeping consultant at Tottenham Hotspur.

RISING STARS

It was a very positive first season for our development squad.

After winning National Group Two in phase one and then the Elite Group in phase two, the lads toppled Everton 3-2 in the play-off semi-finals. Spurs were up against Manchester United in the final at Old Trafford. They were well on course leading 2-0 at half-time but United staged a remarkable comeback to win 3-2.

The team won 17 of 28 matches altogether, losing six in total and just four between 29 August and 20 May. They notched up an incredible 82 goals in that time. More importantly, 18 players who turned out for the Under-21s this season also spent valuable time out on loan.

One match our young side will never forget came at Underhill for the Under-21 North London derby, officially a home game for Arsenal, but Spurs fans turned up in force. At least 2,000 fans made the short trip to Barnet. Nabil Bentaleb's 46th-minute strike secured a 1-0 victory

Captain for the majority of our 2012/2013 campaign. Grant joined the Club from Brighton in May 2012. He is currently on loan at Swindon.

Grant Hall

Tom Carroll

Tom needs no introduction. The England Under-21 international featured in our Europa League campaign in 2011/2012 and last season. Tom made seven League appearances in 2012/2013.

Cristian joined Spurs from Barcelona in July 2011. He was named on the bench for our Carling Cup tie at Stoke in September 2011.

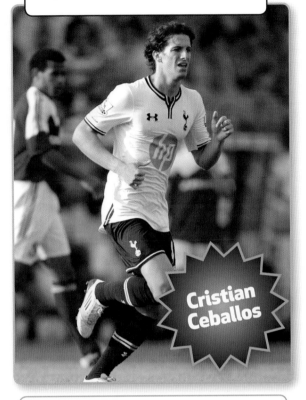

Cristian Ceballos

Ryan Fredericks

Ryan featured in our First Team during our Europa League campaign in 2011/2012 season. His versatility has seen him play on the wing and at right-back during his Spurs career.

Highly rated midfielder joined Peterborough on loan last season. Alex signed a new two-year contract at White Hart Lane during his loan spell. He is currently on loan at Swindon.

Alex Pritchard

Kenny McEvoy

Kenny produced a number of impressive performances for the Under-21 side last season. He received a standing ovation at Anfield after a superb performance against Liverpool Under-21s.

SUPER SPURS QUIZ

It's a grand old team to play for and it's a grand old team to see, so if you know your history, try this 2014 Super Size Spurs Quiz.

1. **Where did Spurs finish in Season 2012/2013?**

   ....

2. Jimmy Greaves joined Spurs from which club?

   ....

3. **Mousa Dembele represents which nation?**

   ....

4. Name our matchday Club mascot.

   ....

5. **Name our opponents in Group J in the 2012/2013 Europa League.**

   ....

6. Name our three Belgium internationals.

   ....

7. **Who were our opponents in the 1981 FA Cup Final?**

   ....

8. Paulinho joined Spurs from which Brazilian club?

   ....

9. **Andre Villas-Boas won the Europa League in 2010-11 with which Portuguese club?**

   ....

10. We beat which Georgian side 5-0 away in the Europa League in August 2013?

    ....

11. **We signed Roberto Soldado from which La Liga club?**

    ....

12. Who scored our Goal of the Season against West Ham in 2012/2013?

    ....

13. **On how many occasions have Spurs won the FA Cup?**

    ....

14. In 2012/2013 we secured a record Premier League points total. How many points did we earn?

    ....

15. **Who did we face on the opening day of Season 2013/2014?**

    ....

ANSWERS ON PAGE 60

PRE-SEASON REPORT

Swindon 1-1 Tottenham Hotspur

Gareth Bale put Spurs ahead, but an Andy Williams goal on 75 minutes secured a draw for League One Swindon.

Colchester 0-0 Tottenham Hotspur

A mixture of First Team and Under-21 squad members were kept out by Colchester goalkeeper Sam Walker as another League One side earned a draw.

Tottenham Hotspur 1-3 Sunderland
Barclays Asia Trophy

We kicked-off the Barclays Asia Trophy with a 3-1 loss against Sunderland in Hong Kong. Gylfi Sigurdsson struck after 27 minutes, but goals from Cabral, Wes Brown and David Moberg Karlsson secured a place in the Final for Sunderland against Manchester City.

South China 0-6 Tottenham Hotspur
Barclays Asia Trophy

Jermain Defoe grabbed a hat-trick as we completed the Barclays Asia Trophy with an emphatic 6-0 victory over South China at Hong Kong Stadium. Clint Dempsey (now at Seattle Sounders), Andros Townsend and an own goal from Tse Sean Ka Keung were the other goal scorers.

Monaco 5-2 Tottenham Hotspur

Spurs were without a number of key players against Monaco but it was an excellent test for the team with match fitness crucial to a good start to the season. Harry Kane and Andros Townsend scored for Spurs.

Tottenham Hotspur 1-1 Espanyol

Roberto Soldado scored a debut goal from the penalty spot in front of a sold out White Hart Lane. David Lopez levelled for Espanyol, but it was a day of positives as Sandro and Younes Kaboul returned from long-term injury lay-offs.

SPOT THE DIFFERENCE

Can you spot the six differences between the two images?

ANSWERS ON PAGE 61

GUESS THE SEASON

In a new feature, we want you to re-live your favourite Spurs moments. But can you guess the season?

1

SPURS 2-1 EVERTON
Jurgen Klinsmann scores on his home debut.

2

ARSENAL 2-3 SPURS
Rafael van der Vaart levels from the penalty spot before Younes Kaboul scores a famous winner.

3

LEICESTER 0-1 SPURS
Allan Nielsen scores in stoppage time to win the Worthington Cup.

4

CHELSEA 1-2 SPURS - AET
Spurs win the Carling Cup after Jonathan Woodgate's extra-time goal against Chelsea.

5

SHEFFIELD WEDNESDAY 3-4 SPURS
Teddy Sheringham scores on 19 minutes to put Spurs ahead at Hillsborough.

ANSWERS ON PAGE 61

GOAL
OF THE SEASON

What a season we experienced for outstanding goals! Gareth Bale's superb stoppage-time winner against West Ham at Upton Park won the award for Goal of the Season, as voted for by Spurs fans on our official Facebook page.

Of the 6056 votes which were cast on our Facebook page, 58.7% were for the West Ham goal while the solo effort against Manchester United received 25.5%.

WINNER
GARETH BALE V WEST HAM

In the 90th minute, with the score level at 2-2, Gareth picked the ball up around 30 yards from goal, turned and hit an unstoppable shot into the top corner.

There were plenty of spectacular goals throughout the season. Here are our favourites.

AARON LENNON V SUNDERLAND

After the ball bounced to Aaron outside the penalty area, he slid past one defender, evaded the challenge of another and cooly finished around Mignolet to secure a 2-1 Spurs win.

GARETH BALE V SUNDERLAND

A perfect way to end a great season, Gareth worked a bit of space on the edge of the box and curled a fantastic strike into the top corner to secure the three points against Sunderland on the final day of the Premier League season.

GARETH BALE V MANCHESTER UNITED

A superb solo goal from Gareth in a 3-2 win against Manchester United early in the season. Picking the ball up near the centre circle, he ran at the opposition defence before slotting a right-footed strike past Lindegaard in the United goal.

EMMANUEL ADEBAYOR V CHELSEA

As the defence backed off, Ade continued his progress towards goal before looping a shot beyond the reach of Petr Cech in Chelsea's goal.

FACTS FACTS FACTS!

Do you want to impress your mates with stats on Tottenham Hotspur? Or do you want to defend them against rivals' supporters?!

Below are impressive facts on our 2012/2013 League campaign.

Spurs' total of 72 points is the highest ever total for a top-flight team finishing outside the top four in a 38-game season. (opta)

Spurs' points total would have been enough to finish in second place two seasons ago. (opta)

72 points set a new Club record for most points in a Premier League season. It was also our best return since earning 77 points in the 1984-1985 season.

Under Andre Villas-Boas, Spurs picked up 34 points on their travels – their best away return since 1984/1985, where we gained 41 points.

Spurs won 10 away Premier League games – the most away wins in a Premier League season.

Both Spurs and Swansea were not awarded a single penalty kick in 2012/2013 – only five other sides have not been awarded a penalty in a Premier League campaign before this season, with the last instance being Charlton Athletic in 2004/2005. (opta)

Spurs scored 16 goals from outside the box (Bale with nine of them), more than any other side. (opta)

TOP SCORERS
2012/2013

26 **Gareth Bale**
21 Premier League, 1 Capital One Cup, 1 FA Cup, 3 Europa League

15 **Jermain Defoe**
11 Premier League, 4 Europa League

12 **Clint Dempsey**
7 Premier League, 3 FA Cup, 2 Europa League

8 **Emmanuel Adebayor**
5 Premier League, 3 Europa League

7 **Gylfi Sigurdsson**
3 Premier League, 3 Europa League, 1 Capital One Cup

6 **Jan Vertonghen**
4 Premier League, 1 Capital One Cup, 1 Europa League

4 **Aaron Lennon**
4 Premier League

2 **Steven Caulker**
2 Premier League

Michael Dawson
1 Europa League, 1 Premier League

Mousa Dembele
1 Premier League, 1 Europa League

1 **Benoit Assou-Ekotto**
1 Premier League

William Gallas
1 Premier League

Sandro
1 Premier League

Andros Townsend
1 Capital One Cup

PAGE 37 TOTTENHAM HOTSPUR ALL-TIME GREATS

Y	H	R	K	T	P	M	B	D	B	K	Y
L	V	E	I	N	R	G	B	N	L	R	O
L	G	W	N	R	A	T	I	I	L	D	P
R	N	O	G	F	W	M	N	N	A	T	E
S	X	L	X	C	K	S	Y	D	O	L	Z
E	D	F	F	L	M	X	L	R	D	L	T
L	L	H	Q	A	T	O	K	D	R	Z	A
I	B	C	N	Z	S	D	O	P	M	E	C
D	Y	N	B	C	P	H	F	H	N	K	P
R	B	A	G	A	S	C	O	I	G	N	E
A	M	L	Q	G	Q	Y	N	K	P	X	N
K	B	B	L	T	T	U	B	B	A	M	D

PAGE 48 SUPER SPURS QUIZ ANSWERS

1. 5th

2. AC Milan

3. Belgium

4. Chirpy

5. Lazio, Maribor and Panathinaikos

6. Nacer Chadli, Jan Vertonghen and Mousa Dembele

7. Manchester City

8. Corinthians

9. FC Porto

10. Dinamo Tbilisi

11. Valencia

12. Gareth Bale

13. Eight

14. 72

15. Crystal Palace

PAGE 52 **SPOT THE DIFFERENCE**

PAGE 53 **GUESS THE SEASON ANSWERS**

1 1994/1995

2 2010/2011

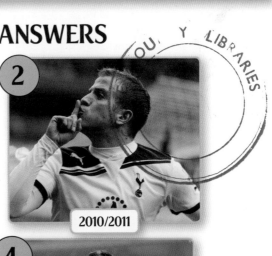

3 1998/1999

4 2007/2008

5 1994/1995

WHERE'S CHIRPY?